EDGE BOOKS™

Kitchen Science

Science Experiments

THAT

FLY

AND

MOVE

Fun Projects for Curious Kids

by Kristi Lew

CAPSTONE PRESS
a capstone imprint

Edge Books are published by Capstone Press,
151 Good Counsel Drive, P.O. Box 669, Mankato, Minnesota 56002.
www.capstonepub.com

Books published by Capstone Press are manufactured with paper
containing at least 10 percent post-consumer waste.

Library of Congress Cataloging-in-Publication Data
Lew, Kristi.
  Science experiments that fly and move : fun projects for curious kids / by
Kristi Lew.
    p. cm.—(Edge books. Kitchen science)
  Summary: "Provides step-by-step instructions for science projects using
household materials and explains the science behind the experiments"—Provided
by publisher.
  Includes bibliographical references and index.
  ISBN 978-1-4296-5426-5 (library binding)
  ISBN 978-1-4296-6252-9 (paperback)
  1. Science—Experiments—Juvenile literature. I. Title. II. Series.

  Q182.3.L43 2011
  507.8—dc22

                                          2010025206

Editorial Credits
Lori Shores, editor; Veronica Correia, designer; Sarah Schuette, photo stylist;
    Marcy Morin, studio scheduler; Wanda Winch, media researcher;
    Eric Manske, production specialist

Photo Credits
All photos by Capstone Studio/Karon Dubke

Printed in the United States of America in Stevens Point, Wisconsin.
0921010   005934WZS11

TABLE OF CONTENTS

Introduction

Scientists use the knowledge of how stuff works to make everyday items even better. Scientists often start out by asking, "What would happen if I ... ?" Then they design an experiment to test their idea. This book is full of science experiments and projects that you can try. But you don't need a fancy laboratory to do them. You can do them in your own kitchen.

When you try an experiment for the first time, it may not turn out the way you planned it would. That's all right. This happens to scientists all the time. And just like a scientist, you'll still discover something new, even if it's not what you expected. Sometimes surprise discoveries turn out to be cooler than the original ideas!

When trying the experiments in this book, keep the following tips in mind. Read through all the directions and gather the materials before you begin. And remember to clean up when you're finished. But the most important thing to remember? Experimenting with science should be fun!

Surface Magic

Here's an experiment that looks like magic. Toothpicks float on the surface of water because water molecules stick together. But add a tiny bit of soap and the surface tension is broken.

What you need:

- shallow bowl
- water
- 5 toothpicks
- liquid dish soap
- small bowl or cup

What you do:

1 Fill a shallow bowl with water. Place one toothpick on the surface of the water.

2 Place a second toothpick on the surface of the water so that one end overlaps the end of the first toothpick. Repeat with two more toothpicks so you have a square with all ends overlapping.

molecule—the atoms making up the smallest unit of a substance
surface tension—the pull on the surface of liquids caused by the attraction of the molecules to one another

3 Use the fifth toothpick to poke the water inside the square. You'll see that the square doesn't move.

4 Pour a little dish soap into a small bowl or cup. Dip the end of the fifth toothpick into the soap.

5 Dip the soapy end of the toothpick into the water in the middle of the square. Watch as the toothpicks move like magic.

Instead of making the square out of toothpicks, sprinkle pepper on the surface of the water. Watch what happens when you dip the soapy toothpick in the water.

Why it works:

Water molecules stick together. That's why it seems like there is a thin, elastic film on the water for the toothpicks to rest on. But soap molecules are different. One end of the molecule is attracted to water, but the other end pushes water away. When you added soap to the water, it moved the molecules around, making the toothpicks move too.

AiR BaLL

Here's a science experiment you can share at the lunch table. Tell your friends you can lift a ball without ever touching it.

What you need:

- scissors
- clear pudding cup, empty
- drinking straw
- modeling clay
- ping-pong ball

What you do:

1 Cut a small hole in the bottom of a pudding cup.

2 Stick a straw through the hole. Seal the hole with modeling clay.

3 Place a ping-pong ball on a table. Hold the cup just above the ball. The cup should not touch the table.

4 Blow into the straw. The ball will rise and spin.

Why it works:

The air you blow through the straw goes around the ball and out under the edges of the cup. But that's not the trick. Air that's moving fast creates an area of low **air pressure**. When you blow through the straw, you create an area of low air pressure around and above the ball. What makes the ball rise? The pocket of high air pressure below the ball pushes it up into the area of low pressure.

air pressure—the weight of air

FLOATING ON AIR

A hovercraft is a vehicle that moves on a cushion of air just above land or water. Instead of tossing a scratched CD, use it to make your own mini hovercraft.

What you need:

- balloon
- old CD or DVD
- pop-up bottle cap from a water or sports drink bottle
- school glue

What you do:

1 Thread the neck of a balloon through the hole in the middle of a CD.

2 Stretch the opening of the balloon over the top of a pop-up bottle cap.

3 Move the cap and balloon to the side. Apply a line of glue around the hole in the CD.

4 Pull the balloon back through the hole to glue the balloon and cap to the hole.

5 Blow up the balloon through the bottle cap. Then close the cap.

6 Put the cap on a flat surface and open the cap. Give the CD a little push and watch it glide.

Why it works:

Air is pushed out of the balloon and flows under the CD. A thin layer of air is created between the CD and the surface. The layer of air lessens the friction between these two objects. By decreasing the friction, the layer of air allows the CD to zoom across the surface.

friction—the force that slows down objects when they rub against each other

MARSHMALLOW SHOOTER

In ancient times, large catapults launched heavy stones to destroy enemy castles. Launching marshmallows is a little less dangerous.

What you need:

- masking tape
- plastic spoon
- wooden clothespin
- marshmallows

What you do:

1 Tape a plastic spoon to one of the clothespin handles. The scoop end of the spoon should be at the opposite end of the clip end of the clothespin.

catapult—a device similar to a slingshot used to launch objects

2 Line up the edge of the other handle to the edge of a table. Tape the handle down. Secure the clip end of the clothespin to the table with another piece of tape.

3 Put a few marshmallow on the spoon. Squeeze down on the clothespin handle.

4 Let go of the handle and watch the marshmallows fly.

For a catapult you can take with you, tape the clothespin to a block of wood. Make sure the wood is at least 2 inches (5 CM) thick.

Why it works:

Catapults work by using **energy** to launch an object. When you pushed down on the clothespin, energy was stored in the clothespin's spring. When you let go, that energy quickly uncoiled the spring, snapping the clothespin closed. Since the spoon is attached to the handle, it moved too, flinging the marshmallows across the room.

energy—the ability to move things or do work

ZOOMING BALLOONS

Who says rocket science has to be difficult? With a couple chairs and a balloon, you'll soon have a rocket racing across your kitchen.

What you need:

- piece of string, about 6 to 10 feet (2 to 3 m) long
- 2 chairs the same height
- drinking straw
- balloon
- clothespin
- clear tape

What you do:

1 Tie one end of the string to a chair. Slide a drinking straw onto the string.

Try using different types of balloons to see which ones move the fastest. Then challenge a friend to a balloon race.

2 Tie the loose end of the string to the other chair. Place the chairs far enough apart to make the string stretch tight. Make sure that the straw can move back and forth along the string.

3 Blow up a balloon, but do not tie it. Instead, twist the mouth of the balloon so no air can escape. Clamp a clothespin on the twist to keep the air in the balloon.

4 Move the straw to one end of the string. Tape the balloon to the straw so the clothespin is near the chair.

5 Remove the clothespin to allow the air to escape. The balloon zooms along the string.

Why it works:

When you blow up a balloon, you force air inside. The air in a balloon is under **pressure** because the sides of the balloon are pressing on it. When the clothespin is released, the pressure forces the air out. As the air shoots out, it pushes the balloon forward on the string. This pushing force is called **thrust**. An airplane engine creates thrust in basically the same way. Air pushing out of the back of the engine causes the airplane to move forward.

pressure—a force that pushes on something
thrust—the forward force produced by the engine of a jet or rocket

LOOPY LIFTER

You've probably thrown a few paper airplanes before. But have you ever tried to make one out of paper loops? This plane may look unusual, but its round wings help keep it flying.

What you need:

- scissors
- 2 index cards
- clear tape
- drinking straw

What you do:

1 Cut a 1-inch (2.5-cm) strip from the short end of one index card.

Try tossing the Loopy Lifter in different ways. Does it fly longer if you toss it with the larger loop or the smaller loop in front? What happens if you turn the loops sideways?

Fact:

The Loopy Lifter is a glider. A glider is a type of aircraft that doesn't have an engine. As long as a glider is moving through the air, it can create lift.

2 Form the strip into a loop. Tape the ends together.

3 Cut a 1-inch (2.5-cm) strip from the long edge of the second index card.

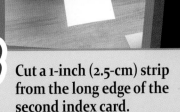

4 Tape the ends of the strip together to form a loop. Tape the small loop about 1 inch (2.5 cm) from one end of the straw.

5 Tape the larger loop about 1 inch (2.5 cm) from the other end of the straw.

6 Throw your Loopy Lifter like a paper airplane and watch it fly!

Why it works:

The loops on this airplane are called airfoils. Because of their shape, air moves faster on top of the loops than the air under them. Slower-moving air creates a higher pressure than faster-moving air. Lower air pressure on the top of the loops and higher pressure underneath creates **lift**. This upward force helps the plane fly.

lift— a force that allows an object to move upward

WHiRLYBiRD

Unlike airplanes, helicopters can fly straight up when they take off. They can also fly backward. That's because helicopters have rotating blades called rotors. Try this experiment to make your own rotor.

What you need:

- scissors
- 2 straws
- clear tape
- ruler
- file folder
- pencil
- hole puncher

1 Cut one straw in half. Place the straw pieces along the sides of the long straw so they stick out about 1 inch (2.5 cm). Tape the three pieces together. This is your launcher.

2 Cut a 6.5-inch by 1.5-inch (16.5-cm by 3.8-cm) rectangle out of a file folder. This will be your rotor.

WHiRLYBiRD continues on next page ⟶

3 Fold down one of the rotor corners to create a flap. Make a second flap diagonally across from the first flap. Unfold the flaps slightly.

4 Place the two short straws near the center of the rotor. Use a pencil to trace around the ends of the straws. Punch holes in the rotor using the pencil marks as a guide.

5 Put the rotor on the launcher.

Try making your Whirlybird using different widths and lengths of paper. Which ones fly the best? Try bending the flaps a little more or a little less. Does this make the rotor fly better?

6 Hold the long straw of the launcher between your palms. Rub your palms together so that the launcher twirls. Twirl it fast to make the rotor lift into the air.

Why it works:

The rotor works in a way similar to the Loopy Lifter. The shape of the wing causes the air above it to move faster than the air underneath. The difference in air speed creates differences in air pressure. These pressure differences create lift. When the rotor spins fast enough, it creates enough lift to overcome its weight and lift off.

Boomerang Roller

A boomerang is a curved piece of wood that returns to you when you throw it. Like a boomerang, this roller will keep coming back.

What you need:

- round oatmeal box
- utility knife
- 20 pennies
- packing tape
- scissors
- two large rubber bands

1 Remove the lid from the oatmeal box. Ask an adult to help you make two small cuts in the top about 1 inch (2.5 cm) apart.

2 Have an adult cut off the bottom of the oatmeal box. Then have the adult help you make two small cuts in the bottom about 1 inch (2.5 cm) apart.

3 Stack the pennies and tape them together.

4 Cut the rubber bands in half. Slip one rubber band through the holes in the lid so the ends will be on the inside of the box. Repeat with the bottom of the box.

Boomerang Roller continues on next page ⟶

If your roller doesn't come back, try tightening the rubber band on the lid. You can also try moving the pennies up or down on the rubber band.

5 Put the lid back on the box. Tie all four ends of the rubber bands together.

6 Tape the pennies to the rubber bands inside the container where they are tied.

7 Use packing tape to tape the bottom back on the box.

8 Roll the can away from you. Watch it roll back on its own.

Why it works:

When the boomerang roller is pushed, the rubber bands twist. The twisted rubber bands store **potential energy**. When the roller stops, the rubber bands start to unwind. The potential energy is changed into **kinetic energy**.

potential energy—the stored energy of an object that is raised, stretched, twisted, or squeezed

kinetic energy—the energy of a moving object

Wind Walker

Here's your chance to power a car with your own breath. Who knew being full of hot air could be a good thing?

What you need:

- scissors
- single-serving cereal box
- 6 drinking straws
- ruler
- 4 hard candies with holes in the middle
- clear tape
- plastic grocery bag

What you do:

1 Cut the top and the back cover off the cereal box.

2 Cut two straws about 1 inch (2.5 cm) wider on each side than the box.

3 Put two candies on one of the straws. Make three 1/4-inch (6-mm) cuts in both ends of the straw. Bend the straw out so that the candies will not fall off. Repeat with the second straw.

4 Tape the straws to the front cover of the box. The straws should overhang the edge of the box by about 1/2 inch (1.3 cm) on each side.

5 Cut the plastic grocery bag into a 6-inch (15-cm) square. This will be your sail.

WIND WALKER continues on next page →

6 Cut two straws about 6 inches (15 cm) long. Tape one straw to the top of the sail. Tape the other straw to the bottom of the sail.

7 Tape the last two straws to the top corners of the cereal box.

8 Tape the top and bottom of the sail to the straws attached to the car.

If you don't have a single-serving cereal box, don't worry. Any small box will work.

9 Place the car on a smooth surface. Blow into the sail and watch the car roll.

Why it works:

When you blow on the sail, you apply a force. Because the sail is attached to the car, this force moves the car forward. To make your Wind Walker go faster, make sure your wheels are moving smoothly. The smoother they roll, the less friction there will be. With less friction, a smaller force is needed to get the car to move. Then you don't have to blow as hard.

GLOSSARY

air pressure (AIR PRESH-ur)—the weight of air; pressure is the force produced by pressing on something

atom (AT-uhm)—the tiniest part of a substance that has all the properties of that substance; everything is made up of atoms

catapult (KAT-uh-puhlt)—a device similar to a slingshot used to launch objects

energy (EH-nuhr-jee)—the ability to move things or do work

friction (FRIK-shuhn)—the force that slows down objects when they rub against each other

kinetic energy (ki-NET-ik EN-ur-jee)—the energy in a moving object

lift (LIFT)—a force that allows an object to move upward

molecule (MOL-uh-kyool)—the atoms making up the smallest unit of a substance

potential energy (puh-TEN-shuhl EN-ur-jee)—the stored energy of an object that is raised, stretched, twisted, or squeezed

pressure (PRESH-ur)—a force that pushes on something

surface tension (SUHR-fuhs TEN-chuhn)—the pull on the surface of liquids caused by the attraction of the molecules to one another

thrust (THRUHST)—the forward force produced by the engine of a jet or rocket

Read More

Cobb, Vicki, and Kathy Darling. *We Dare You: Hundreds of Fun Science Bets, Challenges, and Experiments You Can Do at Home.* New York: Skyhorse Pub., 2008.

Connolly, Sean. *The Book of Totally Irresponsible Science.* New York: Workman Pub., 2008.

Hammond, Richard. *Bright Ideas: 20 Great Science Experiments.* New York: DK Publishing, 2009.

Internet Sites

FactHound offers a safe, fun way to find Internet sites related to this book. All of the sites on FactHound have been researched by our staff.

Here's all you do:

Visit *www.facthound.com*

Type in this code: **9781429654265**

Check out projects, games and lots more at
www.capstonekids.com

Index